CHILDREN
Biblical and Ethical Teaching

E.G. SHERMAN, JR., PH.D., D.S.T., D.A.

Brilliant Books Literary
137 Forest Park Lane Thomasville
North Carolina 27360 USA

CONTENTS

DEDICATION

This book is dedicated to the innumerable children who with their parent(s), relatives and friend have stood at the altar of the Institutional First Baptist Church in Albany, Georgia for a brief spiritual dialogue and inspiration with Pastor E. G. Sherman, Jr.

Over the past three decades, many of the children have completed college, graduate and/or professional schools and are now gainfully employed and actively involved in Christian Service.

It is to all of these participants that Pastor Sherman extends words of gratitude for the opportunity to have been an impetus in their spiritual development.

ACKNOWLEDGMENT

Words of appreciation are extended to the Institutional First Baptist Church membership who, over 30 years ago in the formative yearsof this fellowship, embraced the idea of a holistic worship service.This worship modality was ideal for our modest membership and it provided an opportunity for family worship where the children were a component of the service rather than to be shifted to another setting often designated as the "Children Church". Additionally, this family centered worship would allow the children to observe theirparents in worship and concurrently gleam insights for their religious behaviors upon becoming adults.

I also utter words of gratitude to the AlmightyGod for my longevity as founding pastor (since 1971) of Institutional First Baptist Church. I also expresses thanks to the founding 12 members (all who are now deceased) and acknowledge the lengthy journey that most of the remaining members and I have experienced. Finally, as Pastor, I utter ongoing prayers for the membership as they each commence to undergo decrements of aging, loss of spouses, relatives, and long-time friends. Yet, I cheerfully acknowledge that the Institutional First Baptist membership remains committed to Christian service.

May God bless individually and collective, is my constant prayer.

Pastor E. G. Sherman, Jr.

PREFACE

Over Two Centuries ago, Jesus introduced the idea of building His church (Matthew 16:18). That idea was actualized on the Day of Pentecost when Peter preached the first sermon after the Pentecostal experience and "there were added unto them about three thousand souls" (Acts 2:41). From that outdoor experience, the spiritual anchor of the church was planted and it would expand as converts were added to the embryonic church. Those believers "…continued steadfastly in the apostles' doctrine and fellowship,and in breaking of bread, and in prayer" (Acts 2:42).

From that humble beginning, the church commenced a pathway that included fellowship in homes and the erection of buildings in different locations during the missionary journeys of Paul. Taking a quantum leap from the end of the Apostolic Era to Twentieth Century America, there commenced a massive expansion in both structure and membership of the church. During contemporary times, it is vogue to refer to the mega church, the electronic church, and the small church.

Institutional First Baptist Church fits into the small church category. One advantage of this status is that it promotes family holistic worship. One dimension of this emphasis is the Altar Call for children as a part of the regular worship period. Within this phase of worship, Pastor Sherman presents different topics—some based on Scriptures, others on based Nursery Rhymes, and some on contemporary issues such as violence, bullying, and academic performance in school.

The selections contained in this booklet were lifted from topics used during the Children's Altar Call at Institutional First Baptist Church. Hopefully, this source will be of value for expanding the moral, ethical, religious and social foundation of children.

INTRODUCTION

During my early childhood, I spent much of my time listening to the radio broadcast of religious programs. This was long before television, so I lay on the floor in the living room as I listened to programs that included Charles

E. Fuller Old Fashion Revival Hour, Oral Roberts Evangelistic Crusade,Billy Graham Hour of Decision Crusades, C.L. Franklin LP records, Quartets, and other religious broadcasts.I was particular puzzled by the lack of interest in and appeal to children of these services. For a long time I wondered if God had any interest in children. This quandary was intensified in our hometown *countrychurch* where children were seen but not included in the worship activities. Upon expressing this concern to my parents, they began to teach my sibling and me about the contents of the Bible. Of the many Scriptures we studied in our home Bible study, two scriptures had an enduring impact on me; both as an individual and later as a pastor. They are: "Train up a child in the way he should go: and when he is old, he will not depart from it" (Proverbs 22:6) and "…Suffer little children, and forbid them not, to come unto me: for of such is the Kingdom of Heaven" (Matthew 19:14).

My concern and request that children be involved led to the inclusion of a children's class at the weekly Sunday School. My mother became the first children's Sunday school teacher in our little church and that concern gave reinforcement to many principles, percepts, and facts that we were taught at home.

During my undergraduate tenure, I served as Sunday School teacher for the college students, but the church regular worship procedures allowed for only passive involvement young people in the services. Again,

I reflected on my pre- college days and concluded that "Church" must be intended for adults. I thought that children and adolescents were mere onlookers.

Upon starting my career as a collegiate professor, I found the same practice in the church where I attended. That reality created a spiritual restlessness within me. The Lord must have sensed that cognitive dissonance because I felt the call to preach—a task never to encompass my aspirations or my goals. Yet I yielded to the call, went through the polity of our home church, enrolled in a distance learning seminary, was called to pastor a church and commenced a bi-vocational career.

At last God had placed me in a position where my dream of a family (holistic) worship could be realized! The services included classes for the primary, junior and adolescent groups, a junior usher board, achildren's choir, an adolescent's choir and a children's altar call.

This book is a compilation of some topics used during my ministry to the children and their parents. The book has a three-fold emphasis: to provide for a parent/ children listening and responding to a biblical topic or a social situation with biblical implications; to promote a "we feeling" between both the children and their parents; and to provide motivation for bible study at home since the Altar Service always included handouts for both the children and parents. Prayerfully, this book will be a source to encourage and even provide topics for family Bible study.

Blessings! Pastor E. G. Sherman, Jr.

THE ALTAR CALL PROCEDURE

The Altar Call is included in the devotional phase of worship. It is called by a member of the ministerial staff. In response, the children and their parent(s) approach the altar where the pastor and his clergy are facing the congregation. Upon forming a semi circle around the altar area, two office assistants distribute a copy of the leaflet to be used in the religious dialogue. The pastor will have earlier prepared the sheet. It consists of the subject and references upon which the dialogue will be based. The pastor reads each question and then waits for the altar participates to read the answer prepared for each question. At the conclusion of the reading, the pastor gives brief applications and then all gathered at the altar will sing the children's emphasis song—"Yes, Jesus Loves Me". Afterwards, all participants return to their respective pew.

LESSON 1

Topic—What is the Bible?

Scripture—2nd Peter 1:20-21

Pastoral Introduction—There are innumerable books found in various parts of the world that cover a wide-range of topics and are used for many purposes. However, ONLY one of the Bible, stands alone as God's message to humankind.

1. What is the Bible?

   The Bible is the Word of God that was divinely breathed by God on holy men of God; who spoke as they were moved by the Holy Ghost (2nd Peter 1:21)

2. What is the nature of this biblical writing?

   The nature of the writing of the Bible is God as author and the holy men of God were the penmen.

3. What are the Divisions of the Bible and how many books are contain in each division?

There are two Divisions of the Bible (Old Testament and New Testament; the former contains 39 and the latter has 27 for a total of 66 Books in the Bible).

4. Of what value is the Bible for humankind?

The Bible (" All scripture is given by inspiration of God, and is profitable for doctrine, for reproof, for correction, for instruction to righteousness" (2nd Timothy 3:16)

5. What does the Bible teach about access to eternal salvation with the Lord?

The Bible specifies the way to salvation as noted in Romans 10:9, "If thou shall confess with thy mouth the Lord Jesus, and shall believe in thine that Godraised him from the dead, thou shall be saved."

LESSON 2

Topic—Creation and Human Life

Scripture—Genesis 1 @ 2:1-7

Pastoral Introduction—Genesis is the first book of the Bible. It gives the account of God's creation that covered a six day period, "And God saw everything that he had made; and behold, it was very good."

1. In some academic circles, the theory is taught that the world and human life were outcome of Evolution. Is this view consistent with or contrary to the Bible's account of creation?

    No, Evolution is inconsistent with the Bible's account of both the origin of the world and human life. These two events areknown and accepted by Christians to be the Divine Creation.

2. Cite some biblical references to support Divine Creation.

    Genesis 1:1 asserts "In the beginning God created the heaven and the earth." That chapter, further, gives a daily account of God's activities during creation. Next, Chapter 2:7 contains the act of human life being created. Next, support for creation is found in Ps. 19:1 where it is stated, "The heavens declare the glory of God and he firmament sheweth his handywork." Thirdly, Paul wrote, "For by him were all things created, that are in heaven, and that are in earth..." Col. 1:16.

3. With the existence of just these three scriptures, why do you feel that there exist individuals who cling to the theory of Evolution?

Such individuals may claim to be atheist, identified with an anti-Christian group, or just a follower of some secular aggregate.

Warning to the Evolutionist—"The fool hath said in his heart; there is no God..." Ps. 14:1.

LESSON 3

Topic—Who Is Jesus

Scripture—Luke 2:1-17

Pastoral Introduction—It seems part of human curiosity to inquire about new comers when they move into a neighborhood. Since Jesus was a new person in Nazareth, a small village in Galilee, many inquired about His birth. Sue three wise men of the east. Jesus was born to a virgin named Mary after the angel told her that, "Thou shall conceive in thy womb and bring forth a son and you shall call His name, Jesus." (Luke 1:31)

1. Who is Jesus?

   Jesus is the Only Begotten Son of God

2. How do we know that Jesus is the Only Begotten Son of God?

   The Bible tells us in John 3:16 that Jesus is the Son of God; also Matthew 3:17 supports John 3:16.

3. How did Jesus come to the earth?

Jesus came to the earth as a baby born to Mary, after having been conceived by the Holy Ghost.

4. What date is recognized as the time of Jesus' birth?

   While we do not formerly know the exact date of Jesus' birth, Christians set aside December 25th as a day to celebrate the birth of Jesus Christ.

5. What did Jesus state as his purpose for coming to the earth?

   Jesus said that his earthly purpose was to seek and save the lost (Matthew 18:11).

   Also, Jesus Himself said, "The Spirit of the Lord is upon Me because He has anointed Me to preach the Gospel to the poor; He sent me to heal the brokenhearted, to proclaim liberty to the captives,and recovery of sight to the blind, to set at liberty those who are oppressed; To proclaim the acceptable year of the Lord" (Luke 4:18)

6. Did all of the people accept Jesus?

   Not all of the people accepted Jesus.

7. What does the life of Jesus teach us?

   The life of Jesus teaches us to be: good, truthful, respectful, helpful, dutiful, focused and prayerful.

LESSON 4

Topic—The Danger in Lying

Scripture—Genesis 4:8-9

Pastoral Introduction—Statements are either true or false! There are times, however, when one attempts to include a bit of each, butany deviation from the truth causes the statement to be untrue, or alie.

1. Who was the first person in biblical history to tell a lie?

   Cain, one of the sons of Adam and Eve, was the first person to tell to tell a lie. He lied by saying that he did not know the whereabouts of his brother, Abel. In fact Cain had killed Abel.

2. How did God respond to Cain's lie?

   God told Cain thatAbel's blood cried unto Him from theground and that because of what Cain had done the earth would no longer yield at its full strength for Cain; and that he would be"… a fugitive and a vagabond in the earth…" (Genesis 4:8-12).

3. Who was the disciple that lied about being with Jesus and how many times did he lie about the association?

Peter was the disciple who lied about being associated with Jesus. He actually denied knowing Jesus three (3) times (Matthew 26:69-75).

4. What was the name of the lying couple in the New Testament who lied to Peter about giving the full price of land that they sold?

The couple was a husband and wife team; their names were Ananias and Sapphira.

5. What was the outcome for the four lying persons?

Cain's work was never again fruitful and he became a fugitive and vagabond for the rest of his life. What a terrible way to have to live.

6. Peter's confidence was affected and he wept.

Ananias and Sapphira fell dead at the Apostle Peter's feet.

This topic on lying clearly warns of the danger and immorality associated with such behaviors!

LESSON 5

Topic—Respect Your Parents

Scripture—Ephesians 6:1

Pastoral Introduction—Statements are either true or false! There are times, however, when one attempts to include a bit of each. However, any deviation from the truth causes the statement to be untrue or a lie.

1. What does the Bible teach about the behavior of children toward their parents?

   The Bible teaches, "Children, obey your parents in the Lord, for this is right."

2. What is promised in Exodus 20:12 for those who honor and obey their parents?

   That Scripture states, "Honor thy father and thy mother: that thy days may be long upon the land which the Lord thy God giveth thee."

3. Is there an example in the Bible of a lad who disrespected and even sought to injure his father and, if so, whowas that person?

   Yes, there is an account of a person who was disrespectful to his father and even sought to harm him; his name was Absalom.

4. Was God pleased with Absalom's rebellion against David his father?

   No, God was displeased with Absalom's action and He suffered Absalom's hair to be caught by a tree branch from which he hung there and died.

5. What was David's response upon receiving the news of Absalom's death?

   David was deeply grieved as reflected in his words, "O my son Absalom, my son, my son Absalom! Would God I had died for thee, O Absalom, my son, my son!

Let us remember to honor and not cause grief to our parents; in so doingwe will be lengthening our days on the earth. Also, let us rememberthat we are going to reap what we sow (Galatians 6:7).

LESSON 6

Topic—The Value of Being in Place

Scripture—1st Samuel 16

Pastoral Introduction—In the 1st Samuel 16 is found the accountof the Prophet Samuel's journey to Jesse's house to select one of his sonsto be anointed as the next king of Israel. Samuel, after having seen thesons, inquired if those were all of the sons. Jesse told him that Davidwas away keeping the sheep. Samuel said to Jesse, "Send and fetch himto me." Samuel sent for David, who was at his station, and David cameto father where Samuel selected and anointed him as the king of God's people.

1. Where in the Bible is the account of a younger child being in "right" place?

    It is found in 1 Samuel 16:8-13.

2. Who was the father of this youngster?

    Jesse was the father of this young lad.

3. What was the name of this particular son of Jesse?

His name was David.

4. What was David's responsibility in the family chores?

David was keeper of the family's sheep.

5. Was David effective as a keeper of the sheep?

Yes, David was effective in his job. He showed remarkable responsibility in his assignment as a shepherd. He defeated beast (a bear and a lion) when they sought to harm the family's sheep.

6. What future position was David given by being in place?

Samuel anointed David as the second king of Israel.

LESSON 7

Topic—There is no Place like Home

Scripture—Luke Chapter 12

Pastoral Introduction—Children are reared in various types of home settings that range from mansions to mud huts. There are manychildren who are surviving in shelters for the homeless and otherswho sleep in abandon vehicles. The Gospel Writer, Luke, tells of an economically secure family in which one of the sons wanted hisshare of the estate. The father granted his request, the son left, hespent his funds foolishly, he soon became destitute, his associatesleft him, and he thought about home. He found that there was no placelike home.

1. Where is the Scripture found for thisstory?

   It is found in Luke 12:11-32

2. How many sons did the father in this account have?

   The father had two sons

3. What did the younger son request from his father?

The younger son requested his portion of the family's wealth.

4. What did the younger son do with his money?

   The younger son spent his money on riotous living.

5. What did his friends do when the money was depleted?

   His "so called" friends left him!

6. After many disappointments, what did the youngster do?

   He came to himself and realized that he had a father that loved him. So he went back home.

7. What did he find upon returning home?

   He found a father who welcomed him with love and found that there was no place like home.

Give thanks! For our having a place to call home.

LESSON 8

Topic—A Growth of a Good Little Child

Scripture—Luke 2:40

Pastoral Introduction—a child is born without awareness of expected behaviors; hence (s)he must be nurtured, taught and motivated to become a 'socialized person'. Unfortunately, not all children are responsive to guidance and many will have a blemished social life. The Bible tells of the growth of one good little child. His name was JESUS!

1. Who was this child?

   This child was Jesus.

2. Who was his mother?

   His mother was Mary.

3. Who was his Heavenly Father?

   His Heavenly Father was God (John 3:16)

4. Describe the growth of Jesus.

   He grew physically, spiritually, mentally; and the Graceof God was upon him. (Luke 2:40)

5. What was his purpose while on earth?

   To teach people how to live and be good and prepare to go to heaven when they die

6. How can I serve Jesus?

   By telling the truth, being kind, learning the Lord's Prayer, and attending church services.

LESSON 9

Topic—Love: Words, Actions, Both!

Scripture: Ephesians 5: 1-2

Pastoral Introduction—Some individuals are extremely talkative, with little action to support their words. Others are of few words, but are humane and helpful to others while expecting no praise, rewards, or gifts for their actions. This type of action can occur within a family as seen in this lesson on love, words and actions.

1. There was a mother who had three little boys who each morning and night would say what to their mother?

    The boys would say "I love you mother".

2. What did the youngest son say to his mother one morning?

    He said to his mother, "I love you mother and what time is breakfast?

3. What did the mother say?

The mother said, "Thank you, and breakfast will be ready shortly.

4. Soon another son came in and said, "I love you mother, where is my ball?

    The mother said, "Thank you, and I have not seen your ball."

5. The last son came in and said, "I love you mother and today I am going to help you all I can."

    The mother said," Thank you and you can start by carry out the wastebasket"

6. That night before retiring to bed, each son again said, "I love you mother".

    The mother replied to each, "Thank you my son"

7. Which of the sons do you think the mother appreciated most?

    The mother appreciated the son who helped her themost.

This account of the three boys clearly shows that love includes positiveactions.

LESSON 10

Topic—The Value of Sight in Learning

Source—(Nursery Rhyme—The Blind Men…)

Pastoral Introduction—the story of *The Blind Men and The Elephant* originated in the Indian subcontinent. This story has been widely diffused. It tells of six blind men from Indostan who desired to learn about the elephant. However, their conclusions about the elephant differed because they each felt different parts of the elephant.

1. What is the title of this Indian legend?

   The title of this Indian legend is The Blind Men and the Elephant.

2. Who are the characters in this Indian Legend?

   The characters in this Indian Legend were six blind men.

3. What was the purpose of their trip?

The men went to *see* the elephant although each of them was blind.

4. What is a basic requirement in the learning process?

   The ability to see is a basic requirement in the learning process.

5. What are two other methods by which learning can occur?

   Two additional methods by which learning occurs beyond sight are: direct instruction and personal experiences.

6. Are there times when personal experiences may be in error?

   Yes, there are times when personal experiences may be in error.

7. Cite an example where personal experiences in learning were in error.

   The poem *The Blind Men and the Elephant* is an example of where personal experience led to an error in conclusion.

LESSON 11

Topic—The Need and Value of Study

Scripture—2nd Timothy 2:15

Pastoral Introduction—the parents, siblings and other significant beings in the environment. Through lengthy and structured study, the individual acquires the knowledge necessary for personal survival. This need for and value of study is taught to children in school and in the Bible.

1. In what Book of the Bible is this topic discussed?

   It is found 2 Timothy 2:15

2. What was Paul's message to Timothy?

   Paul instructed Timothy to study to show himself approved...

3. Did Timothy follow through with the instruction?

   Yes, Timothy studied and later wrote two books of the Bible that bear his name (1 & 2 Timothy).

4. Were there other Biblical personalities that demonstrate Christians who studied and followed Jesus?

Yes, the disciples were trained by Jesus although some of them held professional (secular) positions. Two disciples who were professionals are Matthew (tax collector) and Luke (physician).

5. How does Paul's message to Timothy apply to us, today?

Paul's message definitely calls upon us to study in order to be persons who areproperly prepared and who are not ashamed of our work.

Since this message can apply to us in our school work; if obeyed, it will increase the level of our academic performance.

LESSON 12

TOPIC—The Danger in Violence

Scripture—None

Pastoral Introduction—Violence has been and continues to be a reality in human history. The World Health Organization defines violence as "the intentional use of physical force or power, threatened or actual, against oneself, another person... or group." Violence can take on various forms: domestic, religious, and political, in the workplace and cyberspace. Increasingly, violence is occurring in school systems throughout our society.

1. What is violence?

   Violence is an aggressive, hostile and at times a deadly imposition on a person or group.

2. What are some frequently used objects to commit violent acts?

   Knives, pistols, guns and other objects can be used in committing acts of violence. Anything that can be used in a hostile, aggressive manner or with the intent of the user to cause harm to another is considered a weapon.

3. Is violence restricted to just two persons: the actor and the victim?

One act of violence can impact and usually does impact the entire family of both persons. The police, the neighborhood, the judicial system and at times, a funeral director may become involved as a result of the violent actions of two people.

4. In view of the negative consequences of violence, what should you do?

You should avoid playing with knives, pistols, guns and all other objects that can be used to harm a person. Further, you should not seek to be a copy cat or even act like television actors who play violent roles. Certainly, each of you should practice self-control so that you will not commit violent acts.

5. There is a story in Children's Nursery Rhyme entitled, *Who Killed Cock Robin*. It shows widespread involvement in the aftermath of Cock Robin's murder. You might research this on the internetunder the question—Who killed Cock Robin? The first few lines are:

"Who killed Cock Robin?" "I" said the Sparrow, "With my bow and arrow, I killed Cock Robin." "Who saw him die?" "I" said the Fly, "With my little eye, I saw him die." ...

6. In conclusion, we want to value life and not injury others, disrupt our freedom, worry our parents, and not burden the community.

LESSON 13

Topic—The Danger in sharing too much information

Setting—A Nursery Rhyme

Pastoral Introduction—There is a danger in talking without engaging in thought before speaking—especially to strangers. We must think about the hidden motive of the inquisitor. Often information is being sought which can be used to your detriment in the future. The story of *Little Red Riding Hood* is a vivid illustration of the danger in sharing too much information.

1. The account is told of a little girl who wore a red coat and was called by that name. What was the name by which she was known?

   That little girl was known as Little Red Riding Hood.

2. What did she request permission to do?

   She requested permission to visit her grandmother

3. Was the permission granted?

   Yes the permission was granted.

4. Did she meet any distraction on her journey?

   Yes she met a distraction which was a wolf

5. Did she give him too much information?

   Yes she told him where she was going and why she was going there.

6. How did the wolf use the information?

   The wolf used the information to go to Little Red Riding Hood's grandmother house, remove her from the bed, dress himself as the grandmother and await the arrival of Little Red Riding Hood.

7. Was Little Red Riding Hood shocked by the appearance of her grandmother?

   Yes she was certainly surprised by the "looks" of her grandmother. Grandmother looked like an animal (wolf) dressed in grandmother's clothe.

8. Let us briefly talk about the outcome of Little Red Riding Hood's visit!

   Little Red Riding Hood got distracted by talking to a stranger.

   Little Red Riding Hood provided very private information that the stranger (wolf) later use to disguise himself and trick her.

LESSON 14

Topic—The Great Fall

Source—Nursery Rhyme

Pastoral Introduction—People live at different levels in life. In American (in particular), these levels are called classes. There are the lower, middle and upper classes. People's existence in these classes is not necessarily permanent. Those in the upper class can experience a fall. Such was the case involved in the nursery rhyme, *Humpty-Dumpty.*

1. Who is the main character in this nursery rhyme?

   The main character in this nursery rhyme is Humpty Dumpty.

2. Is the character human or fictional?

   The character is fictional.

3. Did Humpty Dumpty seem happy in his position on the wall?

Humpty Dumpty seemed very happy in his position on the wall. He was proud to be on display for all to see.

4. What does this nursery rhyme depict (show) about a person's level of living?

    The nursery rhyme shows the danger in being too proud.

5. How might we fall from the wall of respect, success, and happiness?

    We can fall from the wall of respect, success, and happiness through actions that include: disobedience, disrespect, dishonestydisregarding school work, and doing "bad" things.

6. What does the Bible teach about the danger of pride (sitting ourselves on the wall for all to see us)?

    The Bible warns that, "Pride goes before destruction and a haughtyspirit before a fall". (Proverbs 16:18)

7. Let us read together the account of Humpty Dumpty. Humpty Dumpty sat on the wall. Humpty had a great fall.

    All of the king's horses and all the king's men couldn't put Humpty together again.

    WHAT A SHAME!

LESSON 15

Topic—Telling the Truth

Source—The Nursery Fable—*Crying Wolf*

Pastoral Introduction–Some people receive satisfaction by claiming to be in dangerous situations and in need of immediate help. Owing to human compassion, people tend to respond to the call. When the call is found to be fake, the responders will then ignore future cries for help; unfortunately, they may be real cries!

1. The account is told of a Sunday school class on a church picnic and one young boy who left the group to create excitement. What did he do?

   The young boy cried in a distressful manner, saying, "Some wolves have surrounded me! Help!" he cried.

2. What did the chaperon and student do?

   All of them rushed to help the young boy.

3. What did they find upon reaching the young boy?

   They found him laughing and saying, "I fooled all of you!"

4. Did the young boy repeat the action a second time?

   Yes, the young boy repeated the action a second time.

5. What did the group decide upon hearing the call a third time?

   The Sunday school group decided to ignore the call.

6. Sadly, the youngster was telling the truth this third time and he was seriously injured by the wolves. The boy's group was saddenedby the incident. The Sunday school teacher said to the group, "You see the danger in telling stories; such is the tragic danger in telling lies!"

LESSON 16

Topic—Talents Differ

Source—The Nursery Rhyme—

The Mountain and the Squirrel

Pastoral Introduction–It is a fact that people are gauged by different standards: some according to age, height, education, religious preference, or marital status. Although variations prevail, it is unethical and downright mean-spirited to demean another person just because of his/her difference.

1. What is the basis on which the theme is anchored?

    The theme is based upon a Poem entitled, *The Mountain and theSquirrel.*

2. What two characters are featured in this poem?

    The two characters in this poem are the mountain and the squirrel.

3. What is the name of a famous mountain in the State of Georgia? It is considered a national landmark.

   There is a mountain in Georgia known as Stone Mountain

4. What the basis of the conversation between the mountain and the squirrel?

   The basis of the conversation centered on the size of mountain incomparison to the squirrel.

5. What was the squirrel's reply to the mountain in reference to his size?

   The squirrel said that the mountain was large, but it was no disgrace to be small and to have talents that were different.

6. After reading of the poem, think of some applications like:

   One person may be gifted in an area while being very unsuccessful in another area.

LESSON 17

Topic—Endurance

Source—The Nursery Rhyme *The Tortoise and the Hare*

Pastoral Introduction—The ultimate outcome of a race, a contest or any competitive endeavor is not necessarily dependent on the competitors' speed or strength. Many competitions are won because one has the ability to continue in the process. This fact is reflected in the fable *The Tortoise and the Hare.*

1. Were the two characters equal in the capacity to speed?

    No, they were unequal in capacity to speed.

2. Which one possessed the greater capacity for speed?

    The hare (rabbit) possessed the greater capacity for speed.

3. What challenge did he present to the tortoise?

    He challenged to tortoise to a foot race?

4. Did the tortoise accept the challenge?

   Yes, the tortoise accepted the challenge?

5. What mistake did the hare make in the race?

   The hare stopped to take a nap.

6. What was the final outcome of the race?

   The hare lost and the tortoise won the race.

7. What does the fable signal to us?

   It shows us that the race is not always given to the swift, but to the one who can endure to the end (Ecclesiastes 9:11).

LESSON 18

Topic—Too Encumbered

Scripture—Luke 10:40-42

Pastoral Introduction—People differ in their choice of topics, ideas, causes and problems. This variation occurs even with families as was the case with Mary and Martha during a visit of Jesus to their home. Martha was busy making household preparations for Jesus' comfort during his visit. When Martha complained that Mary was not helping, Jesus sheds light on what things are really important.

1. At whose home was Jesus visiting when he told one of the sisters that she was "…careful and troubled about many things"?

   Jesus was visiting at the home of Martha and Mary.

2. How did the sisters respond to the visit of Jesus?

   Martha became busily involved with household chores and preparing for Jesus' visit, while Mary used the occasion to talk with Jesus.

3. What was Martha's complaint against Mary?

Martha said unto Jesus, "... Lord, does not thy care that my sister hath left me to serve you alone?"

4.   What was the response of Jesus to Martha's concern?

"Jesus said unto her, Martha, Martha, thou are careful and trouble about many things...but Mary has chosen the best part..."

5.   What does this setting at the sisters' home signal to us?

This episode clearly shows that agendas vary among people; even those who are relatives. However, the best agenda includes time with Jesus.

"But seek ye first the kingdom of God, and his righteousness; and all these things shall be added unto you." (Matt. 6:33)

LESSON 19

Topic—Remembering the Dreamer

Source—Library holdings

Pastoral Introduction—The brothers of Joseph called him a dreamer. They also held envy toward him and plotted to destroy him. Centuries later, Martin Luther King, Jr. was called a dreamer. Like Joseph, he was disliked by many people and later assassinated. Years later, King's birthday was declared a national holiday.

1. What national holiday was observed on the third Monday each January?

   We observe the Annual Martin Luther King, Jr. Day.

2. What was the title of his famous speech delivered in Washington DC in 1963?

   The speech was entitled, "I Have A Dream".

3. What did his dream include about young children?

He said that, "One day children would be judged by the content of the character rather than the color of their skin."

4. Did he live to see that time become a reality?

   He did not live to see that reality because he was killed on April 4, 1968, in Memphis, Tennessee.

5. What challenge does that dream present to you?

   That dream challenges us to prepare ourselves to functionin the society as described in the speech. That means thatwe must have:

   - high moral values,
   - a good education,
   - becommitted to a good work ethic, and
   - abide by principles taught in the Bible.

LESSON 20

TOPIC—A Famous African-American

Scripture—None

Pastoral Introduction—History is replete with people who are viewed as famous because of significant contributions to mankind. Those individuals are given labels such as hero, founder, pioneer, and famous. One such individual appeared on the scene in the late 50's whose name was Dr. Martin Luther King., Jr.

1. Are you in school on the third Monday in January?

   No, we are out of school on the third Monday of January.

2. Why were you not in school at that time?

   We observe the birthday of Dr. Martin Luther King, Jr.

3. Who was Dr. King?

   Dr. King was a famous Civil Rights leader.

4. What did Dr. King's efforts accomplish?

   Dr. King's efforts led to the Civil Rights Act of 1964.

5. What are some benefits of that Act?

   That Act brought integration in public schools, equal access to public facilities and new employment opportunities for all citizens; especially women and minorities in America.

6. How did Dr. King die?

   Dr. King was assassinated by a man using a high powered rifle.

7. What should be our view on Dr. King's life and accomplishments?

   Our view on Dr. King's life should include admiration, respect, and appreciation.

LESSON 21

Topic—The Origin of Thanksgiving Day

Scripture—Psalm 136:1-9

Pastoral Introduction—Christopher Columbus is credited with discovering the New Word (later to become known as America) in 1492. However, it would be centuries later before the Pilgrims arrived in America in 1607. Their first year was harsh a nearly a disaster. However, their next year was a bountiful one, so the Pilgrims held a worship period and called it Thanksgiving.

1. What holiday is typically celebrated in America on the fourth Thursday of the month of November?

   The holiday to be celebrated on the fourth Thursday is known as Thanksgiving Day.

2. In what year was this event started?

   Thanksgiving was started in 1621

3. At what place was it started?

   Thanksgiving was started in Plymouth, Massachusetts.

4. By what group was this event started?

   This event was started by a group known as the Pilgrims.

5. Why did this group start the event?

   The Pilgrims started the event to give thanks to God for life and a successful year of harvest.

6. What was the meat served at the dinner?

   The meat served at the dinner was wild Turkey.

7. What was the dessert served at the dinner?

   The dessert served at the dinner was pumpkin pie.

8. What group was invited to share the event with the founders?

   The group that was invited to share the event was the Native Americans who lived in the area around Plymouth.

9. In what year was Thanksgiving made a national holiday.

In 1863, President Abraham Lincoln proclaimed the fourth Thursday in November to be designated as a national federal holiday—Thanksgiving Day.

Happy Thanksgiving!

LESSON 22

Topic—Acceptance

Source—The Fable *Rudolph the Red Nosed Reindeer*

Pastoral Introduction—A favorite children's Christmas Song is the song *Rudolph the Red Nosed Reindeer*. Children sing, draw and even wear protruded red noses as they enjoy the story of Rudolph. However, embedded in the story is a lesson about one's difference being recognized.

1. Who was Rudolph the Red-Nosed Reindeer?

    Rudolph the Red-Nosed Reindeer is a fictional reindeer with a glowing red nose.

2. Was Rudolph originally accepted by the others reindeers?

    No, Rudolph was not originally accepted by the other reindeers.

3. How did the other reindeers react to Rudolph?

    The other reindeers would laugh and call him names.

4. What other negative behavior did they display toward him?

   They would not let Rudolph play in any reindeer games.

5. What life changing event occurred in Rudolph's life?

   One foggy Christmas eve (night) Santa said to him, " Rudolph, because your nose is so bright, will you guide my sleigh tonight?"

6. What was Rudolph's response and the ultimate outcome?

   Rudolph agreed to be the lead reindeer to drive the sleigh. Using his nose to light the way through the foggy night, his name went down in history as the answer to one of Santa's great dilemmas.

7. What does this fictional account of Rudolph's life, highlighted during the Christmas season, suggest to us?

   This story of Rudolph reminds us that we may be the object of laughter, excluded by some individuals, and called ugly names. However, no matter how odd we may be, each of us has a God-given gift that is the solution to someone's problem.

8. What should be our response when we are not celebrated among our peers because of our differences?

   We should remember Rudolph and use our difference to help others.

LESSON 23

Topic—The Christmas Story

Source—Luke 2:1-7

Pastoral Introduction—The Christmas Story is the most frequently told stories of the year. Christmas is the most widely observed, highly anticipated and family oriented days of the year. It is a special time for Christians in that it is a day set aside to celebrate the human birth of the Savior, Jesus Christ.

1. Where was the baby Jesus, born?

   The baby, Jesus, was born in Bethlehem of Judea.

2. Where did his mother, Mary, place the baby?

   Mary placed the baby in a manger.

3. What is a manger?

   A manger is a open box like container designed for cattle to eat therefrom.

4. Why were Joseph and Mary in a stall made for animals?

   Joseph and Mary were in the stall because they could find no room in the Inn and they needed to rest to prepare for Jesus to be born.

5. What were the swaddling clothes that Mary used to cover baby Jesus?

   Swaddling clothes were towel like "sheets" used before milking the cows.

6. What is the place where children are born and briefly kept today?

   The places where children are born today include the pediatric ward of the hospitals, at home and even in pools of water designed to be birthing pools for babies.

Conclusion

   Humans have experienced significant progress since the time when Jesus was born. Let us be thankful for the time in which we are living and remember to make room for "The Spirit of Jesus Christ," in our lives!

   Merry Christmas!

LESSON 24

Topic—The Unblemished Lamb

Scripture—1stPeter 1:19 and Romans 5: 8, 12

Pastoral Introduction—The Ancient Hebrews were aware of their transgressions and sought to make amends to God by burnt offerings and the touching of goats before entering the Tabernacle. After the last person would touch the goat, it would be released to roam in the wilderness which was thought to carry the sins and iniquities of the people (Lev.16:22). Years later, Paul made it clear that the perfect sacrifice, Jesus, was offered once for an efficacious sacrifice (Hebrews 10:20). This prophetic sacrifice was not a goat but Jesus was indeed the unblemished Lamb.

1. What was the method used during the Old Testament era to seek forgiveness for sins?

   During that era the people made burnt offerings such as animal sacrifices.

2. What prophecy did Isaiah make concerning a forthcoming non animal sacrifice?

The Prophet Isaiah wrote, "He was led as a lamb to the slaughter ...our peace was upon Him (Jesus) and with his stripes we are healed" (Isaiah 53:7-12).

3. Prior to the fulfillment of Isaiah's prophesy, what were some of the sacrifices that were made?

   The sacrificial offerings included "...the blood of bulls, doves, goats and calves...ashes of a heifer."

4. Since none of the human efforts were an adequate sacrifice to atone for the original sins and all thereafter. How did God solve the problem?

5. "God so love the world..." (According to John.3:16); and "... in the fullness of time God sent forth his son...to redeem them...(Gal.4:5).

6. What was the fate of Jesus in fulfilling his divine assignment?

   Jesus was crucified, but God raised him from the dead. Then after 40 days he ascended back to the Father (Acts: 1:9). LET US EMBRACE HIS PROMISE (Revelations 2:10).

LESSON 25

Topic—Death

Scripture—Ecclesiastes 3:2

Pastoral Introduction—There is a children's poem that possess the question and response that reads, "…Doctor, doctor will I die? Yes, my child and so will I." This simple question about death is both historic and contemporary. Death is a part of living that is acknowledged in the major religions of the world. Christianity, while teaching the certainly of death (Ecclesiastes 3:2), asserts the reality of a life after death (Revelations 20-22).

1. When did the first death occur according to the Bible?

   The first death occurred when Cain murdered Abel who was his brother.

2. Does the Bible teach the certainty of death for humankind?

   Yes, scriptures in Ecclesiastes. 3:2 and Hebrews 9:27, both support the certainty of death.

3. With advancing medical technology is it possible for people to live forever?

   No, medical technology cannot prolong life forever. Further, the Bible states that there is a time to be born and a time to die.

4. What is the human life span according to the Bible?

   According to Psalm 90:10, the human life span is 70 years. Some people may reach 80 years of age.

5. Since death is unavoidable, what should be the human response?

   In recognition of and preparation for death, the individual should accept Jesus as Lord and Savior (Romans 10:9) and embrace the promises of Jesus to, "Be thou faithful unto death, and I will give thee a crown of life."(Revelations 2:10).

LESSON 26

Topic—The Crucifixion and Resurrection of Jesus

Scriptures—"...and they...led him away to crucify him...and they crucified him" Mt. 27:31,35 "...ye seek Jesus which was crucified...he is risen as he said... "28:5-6."

Pastoral Introduction—The Christian faith is based upon efficacy of the birth, death and resurrection of Jesus Christ. In the fullness of time Christ was brought forth and became the Sacrificial Lamb required for the sin of humankind. To accomplish this act of love (John 3:16), it was necessary for Christ to be crucified. However, as Christ had promised earlier; He would be raised from the dead.

1. Was Jesus guilty of charges presented in the Roman Court?

    All charges against Jesus were false yet he was convicted.

2. Was Jesus aware of the fact that he would be crucified?

    Jesus was fully aware of his destiny as noted in Matthew 26:23-25.

3. What was the fate of Jesus at the "so called" trial before Pilate in Matthew 27:17-26?

   Barabbas was selected for release and Jesus was retained and later crucified.

4. Was Jesus buried in a tomb that he owned?

   Jesus was buried in a tomb owned by Joseph of Arimathaea.

5. When was Jesus resurrected from the dead?

   Jesus was resurrected from the dead three days after his burial in the tomb.

6. Did Jesus dwell on earth any time before ascending back to heaven?

   Yes, Jesus dwelt on earth for 40 days after the resurrection and before the ascensionoccurred, as noted in Acts 1:9-10.

LESSON 27

Topic—The Little housemaid under Duress

Scripture—2nd Kings 5:1-5

Pastoral Introduction–The aftermath of wars often include spoils of both objects and people. This practice dates back to Biblical times. There was a Syrian captain who brought a young female Israelite back with him to become the maid of his wife.

1. Who was the Syrian captain that invaded the land of Israel in 2 Kings 5:1-5?

   Naaman was the Syrian captain who invaded the land of Israel during this time.

2. What did Naaman bring as a spoil from the invasion of Israel.

   Naaman brought a little maid as a captive out of the land of Israel.

3. What plan did he have for the little maid?

He planned to give the little maid to his wife as a servant..

4. Was the little maid hostile or compassionate toward the family?

   The little maid was compassionate as seen in her wishing that Naaman would contact the prophet Elisha who could cure him of his leprosy.

5. Did Naaman take the maid's suggestion and contact Elisha?

   Naaman took the suggestion and his boss, the king of Syria, sent with Naaman a letter to the king of Israel. The letter requested that the king heal Naaman. This request enraged the king of Israel but Elisha the prophet of Israel told the king to send Naaman to him (Elisha) for healing. Naaman eventually followed Elisha's orders and was healed.

LESSON 28

Topic—Jesus and his siblings

Scripture—Mark 6:3

Introduction—The birth, life, and ministry of Jesus is described in the Four Gospels. Only two of them include his nativity: Matthew and Luke while one, Mark, noted his siblings; He named the three half brothers but not the females.

1. Was one of Jesus' half brothers named James?

   Yes, one of Jesus' half brothers was name James.

2. Was James cordial toward Jesus?

   No, James was not cordial toward Jesus.

3. How long did James' negative attitude toward Jesus last?

   James negative attitude toward Jesus lasted until he saw that Jesus was resurrected from the dead.

4. What were some of James new actions toward Jesus?

   James prayed so frequently on his knees that they developed callouses, he wrote a book of the New Testament that bears his name, and he became the elder of the church in Jerusalem.

5. What insights might we gleam from James' actions toward Jesus?

   We should recognize that every person is divinely different and, therefore, seek to maximize our talents.

LESSON 29

Topic—Turning Doubts into Faith

Scripture—John 20:24-25

Pastoral Introduction—There is a customary statement often applied to individuals who are somewhat slow or hesitant to accept a report. They say, "Don't be a doubting Thomas!" However, the fact is that Thomas was a believer. His desire was merely to verify *"for himself"* that Jesus was alive!

1. Who Thomas as referenced in John 20:24-25?

    Thomas the disciple who was absent was when Jesus first appeared to his disciples after the resurrection.

2. What did Thomas tell the disciples that he would require to believe that Jesus was alive?

    Thomas told them that he would have to see nail prints, put his finger into the prints, and thrust his hand unto Jesus' side before he would agree to their account of the risen Savior.

3. Owing to his rigorous demands, what title was given to Thomas?

   Thomas became known as Doubting Thomas because of his demands before he would accept the reality that Jesus had returned from the grave.

4. Did Thomas have the opportunity to determine, by his demands that the resurrection had occurred?

   Eight days later Jesus returned to the disciples and Thomas was with them. After having greeted them, Jesus called on Thomas to conduct his inspection.

5. Did Thomas seem to have some reservations about his requirements?

   According to Jesus' instruction to Thomas, he seemed to be a bit timid because Jesus said to him, "Be not faithless, but believing."

6. What does the account of Doubting Thomas signal to us?

   It shows us that there are many things we cannot see but need to believe. Examples are: electricity, wind, resurrection, and heaven.

LESSON 30

Topic—Memorial Day

Pastoral Introduction—Memorial Day is a federal holiday in the United States for remembering person whose lives were given in defense of America, whether at home (police officers) or abroad (military).

1. What National Holiday will be observed tomorrow?

   Memorial Day is the holiday that will be observed tomorrow.

2. What day of the month is Memorial Day celebrated?

   Memorial Day is observed the last Monday in May.

3. What is the purpose of Memorial Day?

   Memorial Day was established in America to show respect for all members of the Armed Forces, especially those who gave their last measure of devotion by dying during their active military service.

4. Will you return to school on the Tuesday after the Memorial Day holiday?

No, typically we will not return to school Tuesday after this holiday because the school year, in most school systems has ended.

Let us pledge Allegiance to the Flag.

LESSON 31

Topic—Thank you, Lord!

Scripture—Psalm 100:4

Pastoral Introduction—The Book of Psalm is replete with calls for giving thanks. One example is found in Psalm 92:1 which reads, "It is a good thing to give thanks unto the Lord, and to sing praise unto thy name, O Most High." This need to give thanks is also referenced in Psalm 106:1, which reads, "O give thanks unto the Lord..."

1. What should be our responses to the following:

a. For having our parents and other relatives?

> Thank you Lord for our parents and other relatives.

b. For having good health and soundness of mind?

> Thank you Lord for my health and soundness of mind.

c. For having a place to live and not being homeless?

    Thank you Lord for having a place to live and not being homeless.

d. For having food to eat?

    Thank you Lord for having food to eat.

e. For having a school at which to study and learn?

    Thank you Lord for having a school at which I can study and learn.

f. For having a church in which to worship?

    Thank you Lord for having a church in which to worship

LESSON 32

Topic—The Unmatched Dual

Scripture—1st Sam. 16:38-51

Pastoral Introduction—The Bible has an account of a young lad in a battle with an opponent who greatly overshadowed him. He trusted in God and successfully defeated his adversary.

1. Who were the two opponents in this unmatched duel?

    The two opponents in this unmatched duel were David and Goliath.

2. Were the two persons of approximately the same physical size?

    The persons differed in size, one was a little boy and the other one was a giant.

3. What weapon did each person have for the battle?

    Goliath had a sword and David had a sling shot with five stones.

4. What was the outcome of the battle?

    David slung one rock from his sling which struck
    Goliath in his head causing him to fall; David, then,
    took Goliath's sword and beheaded him.

Implications—This biblical account shows that physical size or strength
does not always determine the outcome of a contest.

LESSON 33

Topic—Sibling Rivalry & Too Little, too Late

Scripture—Genesis 37:18-24

Pastoral Introduction—This topic is on the danger of sibling rivalry. It can occur in families of various ethnicities.

1. Name the Old Testament family that had sibling rivalry.

   The family in reference is Jacob and his sons.

2. Did Jacob love all of his sons equally, or one more than the others?

   Jacob loved Joseph more than "all of his children".

3. How did Jacob show his special love for Joseph?

   Jacob gave Joseph a coat of many colors.

4. How did Joseph's brothers react to the gift?

Joseph's brothers were annoyed and plotted to destroy him.

5. What method did the brothers used to destroy Joseph?

    The brothers' stripped Joseph and cast him into a pit.

6. What secret plan did Reuben have to rescue Joseph?

    Reuben planned to secretly return to the pit and rescue Joseph, but the effort was too little too late, because Joseph had be rescued and sold into Egyptian servitude.

LESSON 34

Topic—The Value of Sight

Scripture—Mark 10:46

Pastoral Introduction—The normal person is born with five sensory capacities, one of which is sight. When one cannot see is known as blindness.

1. Who was the man blind that asked Jesus to restore his sight?

   Bartimaeus was the blind man that sought sight from Jesus.

2. What did Bartimaeus say to Jesus?

   Bartimaues said, "Rabbi, I want to see."

3. Did Bartimaeus loose his sight by accident or was it at birth?

   Bartimaeus was born blind.

4. Did Jesus restore Bartimaeus sight by words or action?

Jesus restored Bartimaeus' sight by His words. He said, "Go: thy faith has made thee whole."

Implications—Let us be ever thankful for the gift of sight and be kind and helpful to those without sight.

LESSON 35

Topic—A Mother's Prayer

Scripture—Matt. 15:21-28

Pastoral Introduction—A Gentile woman approaches Jesus on behalf of her daughter who was besieged by an evil spirit. Through her persistence and demonstrated faith, Jesus healed the daughter.

1. What was the nationality of the mother?

   The mother was a Gentile also known as a Syro-Phoenician.

2. What was the condition that plagued the daughter?

   The daughter was "grievously vexed with a devil".

3. What was Jesus' initial response to the mother's request?

   Jesus told the mother that "it not meant to take the children's bread and cast it to dogs."

4. Did the mother turn away or continue her plea?

   The mother agreed with Jesus, but indicated that the "dogs eat of the crumbs which fall from their masters' table. She continued her plea.

5. What was Jesus' reaction to the mother's statement?

   Jesus said unto her, " O woman, great is thy faith... and her daughter was made whole from that very hour."

LESSON 36

Topic—The Ascension of Jesus

Scripture—Acts 1:9

Pastoral Introduction—The Bible asserts that Jesus is the Son of God, born to the Virgin Mary, was offered as the unblemished lamb required to atone for human transgressions dating back to Adam.

1. Was Jesus aware of his ultimate return to heaven while on earth?

    Jesus knew of and spoke about his return to heaven (Jo. 14:1-2).

2. When did Jesus ascend back to heaven?

    Jesus ascended back to heaven forty days after his resurrection.

3. How did Jesus return to heaven?

    Jesus "… was taken up and the cloud received him…" Acts 1:9.

4. Were there any witnesses to the ascension of Jesus.

    The apostles were witnesses to the ascension and two
    men in white apparel said unto them that "… in like
    manner…" He'll return.

5. Does the Bible contain a description of the return of Jesus?

    Saint Paul gives a vivid description of the return of
    Jesus; he wrote, "For the Lord himself shall descend
    from heaven with a shout… with…the archangels…
    and the dead in Christ shall rise first…" 1st Thess.
    4:16.

EPILOGUE

Children are necessary for the continuance of human existence. They are totally dependant on parent(s), other family members, and professional care givers for their welfare. Sadly, history discloses the existence of numerous and inhumane actions toward children.

There was a time when children were sacrificed to idol gods; they havebeen sold as chattel, subjected to child trafficking, and kidnappedand held for ransom. Even in contemporary times, there are numerous atrocities imposed on children. Among the reported ones are inhumane punishment, isolation, food deprivation, incestuous demands, and medical deprivations.

Fortunately, contemporary society has a network of agencies that are child focused. The major problem, however, is the lack of an adequate system for monitoring and detecting the innumerable types and frequencies of abuses of children.

There is a need for a network of social institutions (family,school, church, government and economy) to formulate and implement initiatives that are pro child oriented. The church of which I am founding pastor has a family focused set of services; they includeSunday school classes for Pre-K, Elementary, Junior, and Adolescents,and the worship service is an holistic experience in which the parents and children remain in the regular service. But there is a special time in the service for the children and parents to come together for the Altar Call conducted by Pastor Sherman. As noted in this book, a wide range of topics has been presented to our children/parents who gathered at The Altar Call.

Hopefully, this book will stimulate further Bible study and parental involvement with the biblical and ethical training of their children.

Remember the Biblical Teaching—"Train up a child in theway he should go: and when he is old, he will not depart from it"

(Prov. 22:6) and " But Jesus said, Suffer little children, and forbid them not, to come unto me: for such is the kingdom of God" (Matt.19:14).

Blessings!
Pastor E. G. Sherman, Jr.

FAMILY HOMEWORK AND REFLECTIONS

This section is planned as a partial review of topics covered in this book. Hopefully, it will reinforce the reader(s)' biblical knowledge and concurrently engender a continuing commitmentto morality.

The review topic is from lesson 1 which is,"What is the Bible?" The subsequent questions are not in any particular numerical order of the lessons.

1. What is the Bible?
    - The Bible is called "The Book of _____"
    - The Bible has messages for life and even after .
    - The Bible contains _____Testaments
    - The Bible was written by holy men of God, but they were merely the penmen while God was the .
    - The Bible's messages are profitable for .
    - What is your favorite Bible verse? .
2. _____was the lad who faced and defeated _____.
3. _____ was an half-brother of Jesus.
4. The person who required physical proof before he would be that Jesus had risen .
5. _____was crucified on a cross at Calvary.

6. The brother who returned to the pit to recover Joseph _____
   _____.

7. What animal was chosen to guide Santa's sled? .

8. _____ was the sister that Jesus described as being too _
   _____.

9. _____sat on the wall but had a great fall.

10. What animals did a younger claimed was approaching him?
    _____.

11. Who was in place where his   father sent   f o r
    him? _____.

12. _____The Syrian Captain with leprosy.

13. The mother who begged Jesus to heal her daughter was a
    _____.

14. The mountain and the _____had a quarrel regarding abilities.

15. Three little boys told their mother that they loved but how
    many of them demonstrated their love? _____.

16. _____gave the wolf too much information about her
    destination.

17. In the race between the Hare and Tortoise, the hare lost because
    he _____during the race.

18. The National Holiday that comes around the end of the School
    Year is _____.

19. When thinking about the numerous blessings that one has
    received during   the   year,   the   person s h o u l d
    utter _____.

20. _____ was born blind, sought a cure from Jesus,
    and experienced the blessing of receiving sight.

21. In Mark 6:3 is found reference to the siblings of Jesus; he had
    _____ brothers.

22. There are two vastly different accounts for the origin of creation and human life, one is Divine Creation and the other is _____.

23. _____ an aggressive, hostile and, at times, deadly act imposed on a person or group.

24. _____ the person who actions included heading the Civil Rights Movement and delivering the I Have A Dream Speech in Washington, DC.

25. _____ was instructed by Paul to study to show himself approved unto God.

26. The Children Literature account of the blind men and the elephant shows the value of _____.

27. There was a youngster who requested his father to give him his share of the family assets; the father did and, in time, he saw the need to return home. He is known as _____.

28. What National holiday is celebrated the 4th Thursday in November _____.

29. _____ birthday as observed as a National Holiday the 3rd Monday in January.

30. _____ was the child of reference in the partial statement "God so loved the world…"

31. _____ Christmas is joyfully celebrated as the birthday of Jesus.

32. _____ the place where Mary laid the baby Jesus.

33. "Children, obey your parents, in the Lord for this is right so wrote what person _____.

34. _____ was the first person in biblical history and he was killed by his brother.

35. _____ was the first person in biblical history to tell a lie.

36. Jesus came to the earth as a baby but left after his resurrection by _____.

ANSWER SHEET FOR FAMILY HOMEWORK AND REFLECTIONS

1. Books, Death, Two, Author, Doctrine, Your favorite Bible Verse _____.
2. David, Goliath
3. James
4. Thomas
5. Jesus
6. Reuben
7. Reindeer
8. Martha, too troubled
9. Humpty Dumpty
10. Wolves
11. David
12. Naaman
13. Syro-Phoenician
14. Squirrel
15. One
16. Red Riding Hood
17. Napped
18. Memorial Day
19. Thanksgiving Day

20. Bartimaeus

21. Evolution

22. Four

23. Violence

24. Martin Luther King, Jr.

25. Timothy

26. Sight

27. Prodigal Son

28. Thanksgiving

29. Martin Luther King, Jr.

30. Jesus

31. December 25th

32. Manger

33. Paul

34. Abel

35. Cain

36. Ascension

37.

SOURCES USED

1. The Holy Bible (KJV) .Broadman and Holman Publishers.
2. Martignoni, M.E. 1955.The Illustrated Treasury of Children's Literature. Canada. Grosset and Dunlap, Inc
3. Foxfire
4. Author's imagination

ABOUT THE AUTHOR

Eugene G. Sherman, Jr. is professor emeritus of sociology at Albany State University in Albany, Georgia. His academic credentials include five earned and two honorary degrees. In addition to his teaching assignments (sociology, gerontology, thanatology, religion and philosophy) he held administrative positions.

In 1971, he organized the Institutional First Baptist Church in Albany, GA where he continues to serve as pastor. His religious activities later included Executive Dean of the Albany Center of Bethany Divinity College and Seminary (Dothan, AL)

Dr. Sherman has recently published two books: The Abundant Life: A Biblical Approach, 2012 and BlackReligiosity: A Biblical and Historical Perspective, 2013. His weekly sermons can be viewed on www. biblicalechoes.com. He has been widowed since the passing of his wife, Dr. Dolores E. Sherman, December 15, 2008. They had no children.

CPSIA information can be obtained
at www.ICGtesting.com
Printed in the USA
LVHW101128291222
736096LV00026B/376